T0363640

EQUATIONS OF BREATH

By the same author:

Strokes of Light (2020)
Feathered tongues (2003)
Liquescence (1996)

EQUATIONS OF BREATH

LUCY ALEXANDER

RECENT
WORK
PRESS

Equations of Breath
Recent Work Press
Canberra, Australia

Copyright © Lucy Alexander, 2024

ISBN: 9780645973259 (paperback)

 A catalogue record for this book is available from the National Library of Australia

All rights reserved. This book is copyright. Except for private study, research, criticism or reviews as permitted under the Copyright Act, no part of this book may be reproduced, stored in a retrieval system, or transmitted in any form by any means without prior written permission. Enquiries should be addressed to the publisher.

Cover image: 'Katie's Chair' © Kirsten Biven, 2024, instagram: kirstenbachbiven
Author photograph: Andrew Sikorski of Art Atlier Photo, 2024
Cover design: Recent Work Press
Set by Recent Work Press

recentworkpress.com

The author thanks the following organisations for their support:

PL

To Mark and Wendy

Contents

Part One: To the Reader

To The Reader   3
All My Troubles   4
Nocturnes   6
Clade   7
Broken   8
Lenses   9
Unlocked   10
Abyssal Dream   12
Currency   14
Will It Snow Tonight?   15
Walking by Lake Ginninderra   16
A Zephyr of Albatross   18
Haven in Lost: A Song   19
Amongst the Messy Scrub   22
My Eyes Take Me In   23
How The Plastic Bag Was Not a Crow   24
Brain Septet   26
    1.   Anterior Cingulate   26
    2.   Temporal Lobe   27
    3.   Frontal Lobe   28
    4.   Hippocampus   29
    5.   Corpus Callosum   30
    6.   Synapse   31
    7.   Occipital Lobe   32

Part Two: Patina

Patina   35
Nadya Ngambri—Also Known as Mount Ainslie   36
Cloud Engineer   38
Pocket Wasp   39
Whiff of Ink   40
Bridge   41
User's Manual   42
Twenty Twenty   43
Gladly Beyond   45
Sulphur Crested   46
Binary   47
Sea Level   48
Meniscus   49
Five Quick Steps   50
If Undeliverable   51
King Of Spades   52
You Know What Doesn't Grow Back? Trust   54
Hound Dog, 1953   55

Part Three: Altered Beyond

Altered Beyond   59
Homo Naledi   60
Globe Of Thunder   61
Urchin   62
Structure and Function of the Human Heart—Three Poems 63
   1.   Anecdotes   63
   2.   Pulses   64
   3.   Passages   65
Curfew   66
I Am Not Blank   67
Punctuation   68
Suspicious Message   69
Two Cassandra Poems   70
   1.   Cassandra   70
   2.   God Kissed   73
Kate Bush Quartet   74
   1.   Babushka   74
   2.   Running Up That Hill   76
   3.   Hounds of Love   78
   4.   Voice   79
Ophiuchus   80

PART ONE
TO THE READER

To The Reader

After Rowan Ricardo Philips

I have googled how to build bridges
the emphasis is, I think, on the stretch
from one cliff edge to the other.

But I am less interested in materials
weights, measures of abstraction and gaps
than I am in that sweet distant other.

Sure, I have not scrambled up
that rocky ledge that invites a tether
to an unknown over the rise…

I have googled what is there and so
I know by heart the pixilated tree, the
gathered stones and beyond

a house—at a distance—
also the road: that one you
know, we know: the one that moves between us.

All My Troubles

An Acrostic Poem

As we meet in a library with books I feel I used to own,
Lit from above, light saunters in and falls equally everywhere.
Later, there will be absences where volumes that have been shaken loose have
   left prints on the dusty shelves.

My mother is not there, but neither is she far away:
Yet, she is far away, as more and more she inhabits my crumpled catalogues.

The problem with these nurses is that they are so practical,
Round the table three blink at me, as if I am some unadjusted light myself,
Oozing at them: I must be handled tenderly, or I may burn up
Under their gazes. I feel they see the fine
Blue smoke of my innermost temper—perhaps they have already seen it—
Living in me, playing through my mother, making dust so sky-coloured
   and so
Egg-shell hued that runs through my throat,
Sifts itself there: I am a vessel and it the essence I contain.

Seems the books lean in to listen—almost topple
Expecting the unpardonable grace of women who have seen too much:
Expecting and longing for the opening of their pages.
Maybe I am a vial of blue that their paper recognises?
Even as the nurses start to speak I know the pages are already written,
Documenting the flow and steep forgetting; my mother is so far away.

Sometimes I think of the bend of her back pulling grass from her yellow roses,
Or how she walked happily with dogs at each ankle under the pear trees:

Further back she stirred and stirred black coffee into sugar
And the slow 'think, think' of her spoon as it lit the edge of the cup
Ricochets along my memory as gold as beams of sunset.

As the nurses lay down ordinary voiced news, I feel mum transfer herself to
    me, life powdered into words, her mercurial past,
Weary from the world, while her spun mind makes a waiting room
A hiding place to transform to blue mitochondrial dust which may
Yellow in the light, crushing the catalogues, breaking the shelves down.

Nocturnes

Morning and my neighbor plays Chopin through her open windows
so loudly it tastes of blood. Her speakers blaspheme.

Nocturnes are no longer nocturnes but a series of war cries over the
suburban fence.

As he died Frederic made his sisters swear they would free his heart
from its bone cage so it wouldn't be smothered by earth.

His heart which bolted into a complication of rhythm; flooded his
pericardium.

A bird is freeing the music and it is smoke over the mountain. The
children are stealing the music, they throat it back electrified.

The blue, blue quadratic noise.

Clade

tipped with sharp points
this phylogenetic tree
becomes blooming; ice on breath

boundaries of life are unstable
at this temperature,
everything becomes physics.

a shark is shark-shaped because of ocean
depths, just so death visits like a
friend you missed

and missed and also
can't remember: who draws a circle
on the thermometer.

Death is kind, though their teeth
are black with frostbite, old friend gone
on a boat slithering over ice.

Broken

A Villanelle

'...*imagining the future depends on much of the same neural material that is needed for remembering the past.*'
—Daniel L. Schacter

Tomorrow will be cancelled, it will break down:
can never repeat the window's walled-in view
exactly as it won't be: because there will be no yesterday.

There were photographs of people yet to happen
that happened years ago: shreds of yet-to-be belongings,
tomorrow was cancelled, it was broken

as blank of blankets, bed rumpled
with the imprint of a face I called my own
exactly as it can't be: there will be no yesterday.

This box was full of associations
achy and stickily familiar.
Tomorrow was cancelled, it broke down

the way a car or body just stops working
no more talking or placing that partial face
exactly as it isn't: there is no yesterday.

Light will be worn beige from overuse, air
whipped vanilla-cream that cracks me into now;
tomorrow is cancelled, was broken down
exactly as it can't be because there won't be yesterday.

Lenses

He was a man who looked through lenses, saltwater, sea-glass, things opaque and arcane. Through his wide-angle, sky thick with light, moisture boiled up atmosphere stretched to blue and arched to touch night across the other side.

He taught me how to look at clouds through his polarising filter. Night, I witnessed stars; small girl I was stretched her mind to bend at this sheer oneiric volume of space, a somnambulance of planets, beginning with light, ending with soft fierce darkness.

Those clouds I so loved pointing out, brimming and cooking up over mountain and range peaked and rambled: through his telescopic sight I would see cuppings in them, pools, waterfalls, full landscapes of foam.

Focus falters, but it is only one perspective—our pinhole view of a most enormous vista.

Unlocked

Two Broken Sonnets

In the spirit of *'American Sonnet to My Past and Future Assassins'* by Terrance Hayes

'I will take my mind out of its iron cage and let it swim—this fine October.'
—Virginia Woolf, Diaries, c. October 1927.

One

I unlock myself from the suburban day that is part timetable
part excruciation. The winter daylight sets time aflame as
I unlock this form that has one marble foot painted with moss
and the other submerged in the Pacific, halfway to here.
I unlock and forgive all the trespassing across the person you see in poetry
while some other part breaks into expectation's vault.
I make a choice between what I must do and what I long for
undergoing a transfusion of the senses so that even if trapped
night's own black wing will hover across me, continually refracting
not unlike stars, not unlike those distant suns. One green foot sprouts
promise and the other is a barnacled friend to whales who breach
to throw their sight along curved voltas of beaches

their breath becomes volume and the volume a singing
unlocking this secret: there is no time in the present.

Two

I unlock a transfusion of the senses that breaks the rules:
ventures to smell sweet as fresh shit and the exhalation of trees.
I unlock your thinking to where I take you next, partly
to pasture, plains, swept bushland that scrubs at the horizon.
Unlocked, I am halfway home among the longings I have counted,
whittled back to seven and chosen. One, flight to sky-cap.
Two, reach lung choir. Three, the orange blossom gate. Four,
love skid to ecstasy. Five, finally rested. Six, certain direction and
seven, curiosity fingering the truth. Choices that take flight
and hover with me on wings made of bird-call and hollow bone
keratin and nitrogen, each one distinctly a colour of the past.
All this in a box made of carbon and pressed trees; as light as stars, as
delicate as

acoustics. Enough love unlocks destruction, love's
destruction cannot lock up the void.

Abyssal Dream

A Sestina

Then, in the dream of you where
you bared your own dream and showed
some circuitry of belief that blew
a buzzing-fuse-wire in your mind
and had you dive to a fountain-scape
well down from surface pressure.

Swimming long and low though that pressure
the water a tight squeeze of form where
coloured fish delude the sea-scape
try to fool you until you showed
how we could all be saved, inside a mind
made up of seawater, comfort; a solution of blue.

Here you held your breath; blue
stood out in branches of your jaw and lit the pressure
of your resolve. Breathing was now a mind
invented need, not a biological fact. Where
dream-of-oxygen came true, showed
diving down through reef-scape

on your urgent errand, escape-
certain of navigation though currents blew
us breathless. Finally, you showed
me the thing you covered with your fist, undid the pressure
of knuckle to reveal a jewelled thought. Where
could it be safely put in the sway-salted mind?

Clenched in your abyssal dream, though I did not mind
holding my own breath inside your thought-scape
I saw resolve, the man you were, where
what you cared for most was us, and blew
your own brains from that inter-liminal-pressure:
this is what my dream of your dream showed.

And like film it unravelled and showed
me sitting with your grey self, lost in mind:
that room's neon-gaze, a separate pressure—
you, convinced-convicted in disease-scape
around you adjustable wheel chairs and air that blew
from square conditioned vents and went where?

Pressure in the skull, the doctor showed
where ruptured filaments undid your mind-
Scape into neon sand and just as blue.

Currency

It is certainly yesterday because the fig tree is naked now, the ground is smothered with yellow wiltings topped with frost. Each excited child brings sabres of ice from water bowls and puddles leaving them to liquefy like ideation on the floor. In the nubs of the branches, just where the leaves were released, pulling them in and down, I put my eye against the new folds the tree intends for spring. It is certainly yesterday when the whomping cold bruises us with arctic promise. Summer's figs will never ripen.

Yesterday I remind my mother that the currency changed in 1966. She sits on a green cane woven chair, the velour flummoxed by her bones. She talks to me from out of time. Not even the names of her beloved dogs act as avenues to return her—as if somehow through saying them; Ninus Moon, Boy Jasper, Queilie, Birri, I could call her home.

Yesterday in 1966—when she had the green scarf and left for London on a boat—and lost or misplaced that ten pound note.

Will It Snow Tonight?

They tell me to divert my mother. To say the unexpected. 'Do you think it will snow tonight?' She demands to go out RIGHT NOW, I tell her the story of how bees built a hive in the wall of my friend's house and how the apiarist had to come at midnight, cut through the plaster to remove the whole hive while the queen and all her workers slept. Then she says: '*You don't love me, you can't if you leave me here.*' I tell her how my daughter arrived in my bed at 4am and settled her tiny frozen fists against my neck and twined her tugging fingers through my hair.

Walking by Lake Ginninderra

A series of Haiku

Walking beside
water
tasting of light

*

Wagtail call
a crack in the
quiet

*

Night-swan
neck dripping
sunlight

*

Peewit
black voice
white call

*

Passing family
polkadot
voices

An Ibis stretches her neck
and flies
to yesterday

*

Eastern froglet
reaches up with
her tiny mossy voice

A Zephyr of Albatross

An Abecedarian

An albatross crosses the avenue of air
blue as a blemish on broken sky she
coasts in a cave of clouds
distance down through the dissociated
empathy of space; a
featured favour, free, a
gift of giddy
height. Her wings hope along
itches of icicles
jetsam of jinxes left behind
kind on the solidness of wind that
lends long love to a bird
manoeuvring and morphing,
nearly a notion; nearly a nuance. The
openess of wing, often
played, preened, plumage
quickly and quietly made
ready in repose for this
sonic scene a
tune of wind through barbules to
undulate and ululate the
virgin air brought up to sing
wings wringing the sound
xylophonic in air as this
yodel yeets into space, along the length of the
zephyr of ozone under her.

Haven in Lost: A Song

One

A lost thing is only a missed thing waiting to be found.

A lost thing is only lost once it is missed and cannot be found.

A missed thing is not always lost. *(Check your pocket for your keys.)*

To be found a thing could first be lost.

A missed lost thing can be found.

A lost thing, found and then lost and found once again.

A missed thing can be found but still be lost.

Lost things can stay lost.

Missed things, stay missed.

Found things need tight-hold to remain found.

Two

A lost yak wool scarf is only a lost yak wool scarf waiting to be found.

A lost expectation is only a lost expectation once it has been missed
and can't be returned to.

But a missed chance to see the family is not always lost. (*Check your
pocket for your phone.*)

And a lost temper can often be recovered.

A missed streak of sunlight can be found again (*once morning comes*).

And when the handpicked book that smelt of vanilla is snatched, it
finds other fingers to follow its lines, then pass it on.

We miss the gentle song the pardalote sings to his wife all afternoon.
(*One-two-two, one-two-two.*)

A house that burnt down can stay lost—even when it is rebuilt.

And smoke can obscure the summer sun—if not its heat—and we
come to miss it like we miss the sound of flowing water or the call
of an owl in the deep night.

And there you are, wearing that smile you never put down. We hold
you, we burn this moment into our lives.

Three

Six lost teeth are not missing in action. Now this smile has new angles
and there are crescents, white among the jewelry.

And, when she is missed each day—though she is gone—she is not lost.

We can even miss ourselves before we learned love as a measure of
distance.

While experimenting with reach we find our toes have come to be
untouchable.

We miss our lost future, though time's tangled promise can still be
found.

We miss the brush of a hand against ours, the lost connect, the
recharge. But we find the words to tell how we lost and missed.
We have them at our fingertips.

A sugar-skull calavera glares out at us from its lost fiesta eyes.

While freedom can stay lost. *(Check your pocket for your ticket out of
here.)*

It's true a missed blank page is always on the underside of the one just
used. Until it is filled.

Hold these moments tight like these losses you found again and never
want to let go.

Amongst the Messy Scrub

The afternoon light
feeds the eye
falsely

her hat's shape
macros in
until the very detail
of time
collapses to colour

anemone and fern are brushing
your tastebuds
green as well as red
taking you to dreaming.

My Eyes Take Me In

After Jaya Savige

An opening, a Pepper's ghost refracted
in mirage quadrupled
the underside a colony of star ascidian

I'd never seen anything so
impossible, I'd know it like
the back of my eye.

Slits in the water like open sky
and like my grandfather I
believed that trees made the breeze

throwing armfuls of air in the, well
space between themselves,
then intentionally toppling.

Remembering locks on trigger;
if it falls on no-one is it still a tree
with possibilities branched

between the many-words-theory
convex in full retinal display
as a measure of optical reflex?

How The Plastic Bag Was Not a Crow

It was not a crow.
Though waving. Though glistening.
Though waving and glistening on the road.
It was not a crow. Though the overing and overing
of black was like a crow it was not a crow.
Though the striking of the light was slightly bluish,
the moving of the bag in the breeze quite birdish
it was not a crow.

In the sun, in the glinting
Of the bag its wrinkles looked like feathers
for a moment
the bag's crumples looked like a crow, broken by wheels.

I drove past slowly
hoping it was not a crow.
I was glad to see that although
the plastic bag did seem to have something inside it,
I was fairly sure it was not a crow.

And I left it there, being not a crow
—continuing to be not a crow—
waving its tentacles in the wind
looking a little bit like those bluish feathers
that crows so carefully preen…

And I risk my life in the traffic
to write how this plastic bag wavering in the wind
stuck down by the weight of something it contains

is not a crow.
And I drive away a little faster now
thinking when I next come back, the crow
might be hopping across the road seeking
to see what's in the plastic bag, that tendrils
it's feathery contents all over the bitumen
glistening a little in the sun;
– a bit like the feathers of the Crow.

Brain Septet

1. Anterior Cingulate

The part of the brain associated with attention,
reward anticipation, decision-making, morality and
emotion.

I am left with a mouthful
of sudden prayers and
your body like a sketch; a shorthand;
the lyric of your wrist; shy of your mouth;
your ukulele hips;
sea-pool-green of your eyes; the whirl of light.
I cannot bear it,
but I do. I will need to walk
out of this room where you stopped
breathing.

2. Temporal Lobe

Responsible for hearing, language and memory.

The students are taking notes; making a mist with this must of their breath. In the crowd she appears tall, soft faces all around, the dumplings of her cheeks, her hair the colour of post-it notes. There may be a bus coming, or a spaceship taking off into the eternal; celestial transfer just a comet away. The man in tinted glasses bows for the crowd, his moustache is perfect over the 'o' of his mouth, but his sideways eyes tell he is thinking of other things, reaching ringed fingers that spread in the exact manner of wings angels carry. It's 2022 and we still don't know what to believe in.

3. Frontal Lobe

Responsible for movement, problem solving, concentrating, thinking behavior and personality as well as mood.

Everything is a memory charm.

Open doors lead
                    to open doors lead
                                        to open doors. The urn in
the shape of a small dog with a belly full of sky, a cup and saucer
looped in a pattern has a blue chime and a trace of Lapsang
Souchong. Walking on a beach one summer morning and you
said look, look at the rift of waves and the way the sea goes
violet at the horizon after morphing through every shade of blue
imaginable: remember this.

And I did.

The scent of your jumper unravels me.

4. Hippocampus

The hippocampus is part of the limbic system and plays important roles in the consolidation of information from short-term memory, long-term memory and in spatial memory that enables navigation.

Doubled white in its curve moon-landed there in the mind.
You would comb my coils of hair and they trickled right down

all the times shadows made faces on my wall
laugh-nodding among feathers of light
I pressed my face to yours—there's a photograph of the moment,
smoked-breath prickled exhaled above my head—bitter warm
curved light tangles fell from me, exactly,
moments placed sweet wet moonshine strains

maps of the left and the right, where the threading leads
back-to-front and sidelong.

5. Corpus Callosum

Is a large bundle of fibres that connect the left and right hemispheres of the brain and carry information received in one hemisphere over to the other.

It is not
the exact graphite
scan:

but the dark cupping

hippocampus
sleeping deep in limbic hold.

Is not the triangle—
your knee under
blanched sheet

but a blank

crumpled ghost
settled there.

It is not
doctor after doctor
who cannot see
what confounds

but you
you who knew the name of every bird in every tree and the tree's
    name, too, its character and likely growth
who now cannot find us here.

6. Synapse

In the nervous system, a synapse is a structure that permits a neuron (or nerve cell) to pass an electrical or chemical signal to another neuron or to the target effector cell.

These synapses snap-static and a radio retunes itself to a station where rambling avuncular anecdotes are read through in random order: hazy, hastily developed. Some are thick and gelatinous, glide-slide and glue easily together. They gather glitter grains.
    Itchy.
        Tinkling.
                Smell like hot prickle-touch.
Stretch and stretch and static-snap.
Rain along the line.

They are made of nothing better than themselves;
of gaps in the searchlight;
of all the grind-grime…
deep-listen for connection.

This static is a void; a void is a thing that keeps itself company in its emptiness.

The broadcast voices speak into void, give hiatus a name. Mind the gap; they speak from the place of no coincidences, just deja vu. Surprise, a delay sliding out of something broken. Re-thread that synapse to fire anywhere.

7. Occipital Lobe

The visual processing area of the brain. It is responsible for visuospatial processing, distance and depth perception as well as object and face recognition.

My sight popped macro
everything edged in exact,

I glimpsed a woman undress through her curtain;
a bird take to a cloud 700m up;

a glance magnification
every dust mote was a fibre of the world's fibrillation,

twirling shape in layered sunlight
exact in symmetry

$50m^2$ of space grains
particular to pollen sequenced in rhythm.

I blinked, looking to you
saw the jewelry clotting on your mind;

a star on the brainstem,
and plaques affixed across intricate neurons.

PART TWO
PATINA

Patina

Voice rain clean as
light fork storm
bubble up earthing needs
shielding into the stream
fits inside thunder.

Light through green-leaf, cloud blades
soaking hearing
timbre damp sweetness
passing time urgent song

mossed in wrinkles
vibrating high that listening
strains not to miss
this pipsqueak sound

as it spends its song-time
water all its passing
ear catching wet filigree

raincloud water's muster.

Nadya Ngambri—
Also Known as Mount Ainslie

There is reason
walking together
through rain–glitter

pausing to listen: frog's
separate voices, children, too
who have grown beyond

they do keep
doing that and doing it
again;

crisp yellow flowers come out of hiding
butterflies sky roam in strata.

We keep learning how to be with this:
tiny prints of newly hatched
tortoise wades wet soil;

feel it as leaves let go from white trunked trees
whorl our tracks; the lizard family in the stallion log,
black ants with eyes like night rain
as storm turns in on itself.

Voices inhabit wind;
song the kind to
listen and it's there

stories-long
startle clear…

        as if whispered
        right down into bone: teachers
        parted world
        unfolded in themselves.

There it is, scaped.

Cloud Engineer

The cloud engineer considers deletions to make space for the update. Watch it age, flutter on the motherboard. Tidy itself invisible. Put under lights it reveals spinning sound only, calling itself a name. *'Everything has layers,'* you say, *'Everything has edges.'* But I have become uncertain about everything. What have we lost here? Wake your screen, see all the data points built into the hard frame; the malware hasn't blotched them. The clouds are still vapour; watch it rain.

Pocket Wasp

The phone gives access to on-screen sorrow. Out over the landscape, a highway yarns through bladed grasses, a live mud-map the GPS cannot make sense of. If only the shine would set itself to night-mode and cancel all calls until that twisting road beats itself to the horizon. If only this spiritual hardware wasn't so smooth to touch, so comforting with its weight-pull on clothing. Its tolls spur action, promise to solve all the fraying problems lurking in the side turns. It trembles like a sleeping child. It buzzes like the wasp buttoned into a pocket.

Whiff of Ink

For a long time I have been breathing with my heart. I have only just learnt that was the wrong way to do it: a flute teacher once showed me how to swell my belly with the fill of air but I simply never believed her and went on playing beat by beat until the blue tinge crept into my skin changed to octopus through the water the exact shade of rock ledge orange-glow of syphon and the whiff of ink that thickens water the way sunsets thicken shadow your hand thickens in mine a receipt for knowledge only we can know because my lungs never stood a chance with their flimsy frilly alveoli if music was reached for by hearing the strains of fluting silence must be bruised.

Bridge

A master engineer sees possibility for bridges everywhere: along stair rails; between the looming rectangles of the buildings; in graphs of where the money you lost went; across from one hospital bed to the other where sheets would suffice as arches and pivots and the legs—though they roll—would be pillars enough to hold a body weight. She sees the equations in the corner of her eye like a glimpse of her own eyelash—how they curve. She watches as student after student climbs the spiral that lets them across the flow of traffic that would not stop for any one of them alone. She has learnt not to try to explain that she can also see the way each man-made bridge is crumbling; how time eats them. There is no doubt they will collapse, implode and she can see them stutter down to nothing but a dusty residue. That she knows that impending date is her pain alone. A silence as exact as a number.

User's Manual

Underneath the skin there is grill. Charming in its certainty of circuitry, mitochondrial motherboard. Water resistant, not quite waterproof, hack is not to leave it submerged for hours so it swells stops all functions. Under the grill there is stuffing, slipping across and between a structure of bones and adjustable cartilage , polymer muscle the fine wires of nerves, strip them back and they have fibre to the node on each joint and each entanglement—pinch out for a closer look. If your screen is current, you can access a database, replay in endless binary the nightshade zeroing of autocorrect—re-live a corrosion of cluster clotting on the data, warping it, even though it is soundproof and generally heat resistant.

Twenty Twenty

made of lobes
such six leaf clover
brain, lungs, ears

think in earthed—
seemed storm was coming
turned out just to be dusk.

(cockies were screaming
to invite dark down;
currawongs sweeping

song across skyline:
dark could come anyway)
Clouds all lobes

kissing closely; trees too,
leaf after leaf
embrace whole cities, countries

map impossible vision
contour lines on all
the antigen-sticks

know bodies as part of swell—
made-up figure time—
hold to this ball of life for a while,

contain it downplayed
lobe following lobe,
immune fold down

pregnant with malignancy
breathe it day follows suit
deadly unthought

learning to trace
a meme to its cohort
DNA wormhole to the next lobe

might kill there, might storm
with screaming white angels
and the fever at 39o

dusk or birdcall
virus inflame
breath—lobe lobe lobe

measuring by distant telegraph
climbs lip to limb
and makes deadly air.

Gladly Beyond

A Golden Shovel

'Nobody, not even the rain has such small hands.'
—ee cummings, 'somewhere i have never travelled, gladly beyond'.

when touched anguish evaporates: nobody
feels the matching heft of it, not
lovers or friends who even
try algorithms to measure hypotenuse; make calculations on the
breadth and circumference of rain
that slants down diameters of space and has
cheek traced a tear-track; an ache of the heart advancing, such
a ridiculous beating it gives the body and so small
are its contractions—an unplottable loss, cooling in our hands.

Sulphur Crested

The man on the white cockatoo raises his hand in salute as if he's remembered something and is about to speak, but the bird shatters the world with its screech and alters our DNA. Our eardrums flicker off and on and off and then there is nothing but silence. The sulphury crest on the beast is enough to blow your eyeballs out and its beak a thousand razors long and curved, a scimitar. As it opens that beak to draw in the air you can see the nub of is blue-dry tongue, berserk in the pipe of its throat where it holds the gift of a voice that stops time. We can tell even from this distance, the man is little more than a relic, the feathers on the bird outnumber his personal insights five hundred to one. The man is grasping the huge bird between his knees, or maybe it has inserted itself under him, there is no exact telling, and no formula that will answer this question. As we wipe the blood from our necks—the trickle falls from our ears—the cockatoo pulls open the fan of both its wings and takes up flight.

Binary

I imagine you drilling down/ into the lion's decayed tooth/details of shade patterns on paved footpath/layers of evening drop their latest track/ later the dog with one ear skewed/ will trot after the girl at the next table/across night's long grass/there is no binary to footstep/ the opposite of pain is stretched asleep on the table/ the lion's appetite is for his keeper/ the keeper pretends not to know/ my appetite is for your air/ quizzical like a lopsided dog/ you pretend not to know/ lay down your body/ like a sunset/ like a footfall

Sea Level

Tide is rising beyond the sandbags though there is still the yellow screech of birdcall—slowed down it resembles whale song; old unmanned tune. Speak politely and circuitry files for kindness, translates the constant flow of data maps accurately. If not, transliteration gives you cockatoo pitch, sulphur on eardrums: an awful guitar solo—tuning-up amps slipping sound over the waiting audience: a misstep, machine torture. What is coming? Horizon caught fraying, this beast is manmade, marches on spindly lupine legs: the tide is rising over the circuitry.

Meniscus

for Giovanni Andreoni

He came for song. He came on horseback. He was a man whose smile extended from the curve of his mouth to curl of his foot. Somewhere on the plain a wind blew off his hair. His eyes were black. He sang as he rode and his voice was a clear morning. He was only there for song: wind, horse and depth of smile were additional extras. He unbuttoned mushrooms; he swore like a pirate; he rode his horse into the house; he lay on the floor with the youngest child and listened to flies. He made room where there was no room before, licked garlic from his palms. One year we gifted him a green bottle of olive oil. He watched its tides. Each time he came in he left his hat by the door. One day, he told me, he ran his palm across the top of the water and felt that fascinating edge of translucence where water began, air ended. There, in the place where his palm couldn't rest. There, he said, was the song that he had come for.

Five Quick Steps

Dog runs forward into room that smells dark. There is a figure that rises from bed, a red striped blanket falls aside. This man is not my father. Dog takes five quick steps into room, crossing floor; but as the man rises, she smells he is not my father, a man we both loved. In this room he is lost. To us. To himself. He is a crater that he fell into. There are curtains over his eyes that are not cataracts. There are cataracts between him and all our past. So, dog, knowing with her nose, veers aside, turning last minute, scratching tiles with her toenails, pretends it was bed-leg she was interested in; this red striped blanket that smells gone.

If Undeliverable

The hour where they throw
voices out into the sky:

rest them where they land,
in among the grass or twigs,

ready to be collected first thing in the morning.
If undeliverable please return to the third branch, second twig.

If undeliverable, owl will.
If undeliverable, hold onto it yourself.
Sunset after sunset after sigh.

King Of Spades

My friend—who resembles the king of spades
queen's slipper edition
but without that quilted beard—
calls from out of time.

She says: 'People die. My father was just one of them.'
But, there is nothing more personal than death,
even if my friend's bladed eye and quivering
ski-jump nose gave her away.

These old limbic friends
with their harrowing deliveries
of blood-to-the-head.
Once, I thought her intelligent enough

to get away with murder;
she'd probably have chosen me,
with Macbeth precision and her royal eye.
But I also knew she had an underside,

that coupled twin lurking under the doublet,
his beard blanketing the chest full
of salty crystals and snoring dogs.
Death is all about you.

Birth, it's really about your mother.
Her mother folded her birdy hands—
napkins that frighted so easily into
getting things sorted.

Laying out sandwiches
while also playing the oboe: finger joints
like flight feathers, tips curving up.
I may have imagined the funeral.

People die. All the time. My friend sat as still as her portrait;
her hair was exact.
But, I could hear the salty shake of her precious stones,
the muffled waking yawns of all those dogs.

You Know What Doesn't Grow Back? Trust

She tells me she doesn't trust him; letting her imagination out on the
    longest lead she has—
it still tugs forward. A ribboned stretch spooled out from her revolving
    wrist.

Imagination wants the shadows tonight, blue sharp angles of the
    building's corners,
everything unfamiliar in the moon's wafted light; a whole reflected
    city posed in the water; a

stream of lights along the bank of the lake.
Imagination, dark-shaped small all mossy tufts of fur hurls forward.

A pull, and it is caught.
She does not trust him: meaning, she trusts herself. Trusts herself
    enough to not trust him.

Such marvelous shimmers of light in the water—
follow the ribbon to imagination's kill.

Hound Dog, 1953

And Big Mama Thornton is singing out about a hound dog: note that the reminiscent moon has shot stars one by one over huge distances and no longer are they stars, but holes in the sky. Listening to her voice is like listening to the real thing when all you knew were story-holes: listening to her song is like hearing true activity when you were sold on a substitute: listening to her song is like hearing the holes in the sky sing through the holes in the sky. Hearing that song sung by that woman—when all sound was scratchy and all colour leached out sidelong from the process of time—is like watching the moon get out her gun and shoot them all out, every one.

PART THREE
ALTERED BEYOND

Altered Beyond

Limit of breath,
here threadbare
teased apart
sunlit surges
through spaces
fashions vibration-coffins
passing seconds
unrequited breath-equations.

Grey-area system magnifies
extreme pixelations
words are fatigued before they are fertile
burrow down eons of DNA code
spin and ordinary: how shadows fall, how days take
nights to unfold.

A single neutron
transmitting
webbed-woven blaze
of sense
shadow come to life.

This dry dust was once lumens
one photon of yourself,
elevated to travel
morphing trail
spatial in matter
nothing is ending,
just altered beyond.

Homo Naledi

'Homo naledi, an early human ancestor, intentionally buried their dead and made crosshatch engravings in the cave walls nearby.'
—from an article by John Hawks of the University of Wisconsin–Madison.

Water bared me out of hiding, bones laid out by tides that flew fast across surface, fell slow on depth. Look at my ovoid skull half haloed by murky light; a bowl of moon-dreamed condition phasing through a lifetime of not drowning, then to drown. Frayed at my finger webbing, my skin a nibble for fish, so. The milk tone of metatarsal, the rings of my teeth, fibia fragments, canals of bone, now volume of what once was mine gone, stirred gently into black ocean sand.

Making the passage through the stone, between the slither of cave, under the world's backbone, in the human-cradle light-led to feel the scorch of grief, enough to ring the blank wall with hammering.

Memento against the still dark.

Globe Of Thunder

Not a lover but a through way, trajectory, froth cold. Wasn't worth trouble or cost. Found at The Crazy Horse whistle-whinnying enough to make real nightmares. The stallion bolted. His tunnel of breath. This inner ambit: globe of thunder; hoof on my clavicle.

Folded hands keep him awake, dusting the hours feather breathing too light shallow too hang-below the edge fall, eavesdropping fragile even as huge arterial flow. Bang of cardiac. Night crawls past why this pulse, why this chestnut?

Eating the times breakfasting on air light is what broke in and stole door lock, no knocking, no entrance exit. Pure and over. Neighing the distances.

Urchin

The skull-cave underside splits zagged in urchin-shell. Here sections are wheeled out, spoken, pronged with distance, balanced long divisions, exact. Above they balloon in bone; iridescent as abalone, pearl's own opal mother. Lived longer than recalled; a paradise pooled here, where synapse strings of sleep bubble across, tentacular, teetering on light. In this sea egg, an oval white house with two windows, one door. The roof is low, but refracted these dreams are to die for.

Structure and Function of the Human Heart—Three Poems

1. Anecdotes

If river has an anecdote for you it is a hazy brush stranding across the quag of land and making this for itself, a way of water—sweet clean wetness, perhaps, that takes itself with itself down gravity's channel. It seems water is cleaner than air, through it pebbles are magnified, bright and collectable, suddenly more than the grindings of the last ice age. River tells you stories, its own night-song. Everything else has quietened but long song of water going past continues. It always did, even in dust times when rain forgot to rain, river, invisible, still slithered.

If blood has an anecdote for you it tells you in a constant soft warm bang, veining across and through the quad of body; pushed to flooding by invisible electric life, bashing against gravity, going down arteries up veins down arteries exactly as living demands— while carrying everything for body; for life and thought and with this magnifying being alive until it is easy to forget that living is not collectable, that bodies are made simply of the grindings of the last ice age. Blood tells us this story: when everything but our thoughts are still. Telling what we made ourselves from; what we treasure with our limited warmth. Even with disease and dust that clogs our lungs, blood says go on living, as if nothing had happened.

Forgetting has an anecdote: absence, hiatus, space where there was something and then, nothing is there again.

2. Pulses

Listening to coursing: no light to recover from imagination's bridges swallowed by the flow. Swallowing landscape, everything even sounds low—tone of unfamiliar. Pressing from left ventricle to the great gathering of fluid pulsing by carotid and slipping by this ear. Nightly arterial pressure, passing though places at once known and unknown. A great weight and migration of it, waxing the shore, passing all known markers, collecting a slippage of syllables vanishing and intricately drowned. Listening to the flow in the dark, press hearing interior, dark fingerprints hollowing the littoral.

3. Passages

In these four chambers the soundtrack is constant rush, full of plosive and sibilants that if listened to long enough would surely sing all the songs ever known or invented by man, woman, non-binary, machine, animal, bird. There! Long slow songs of whales, or is it a high whistly tune of feather-covered birds? Perhaps it is all a rustle of fabrication? Poised here on the septum-bridge, watching this river mark time with high low singing. A turtle sings along with the washing machine. A frog makes a tune a phone longs to master, promising with beep-beep-beep love and life never ending. By the red and brown smooth stroke of vibration calms us to nothing, where breath lives but cannot sing along.

Curfew

A curfew has been called on reflection; until further notice all shadows are grounded. Catalogue your dreams, submit them to the panel. Feel them throb through their shells: a regular patter of ecstatic song. Sunlight bursts and puckers R.L. breathing takes up space, but someone needs to do it. Each breath a loop-de-loop, present in an uncanny valley between here and now. When thinking becomes banned, imagining is a fineable offence, we'll all be stuck on screen binging on fillers and sawdust and hype.

They tell you not to eat any foodstuffs your great grandmother would not recognise. But, they haven't thought to say that when you turn the light off, think of her resonating with the times: she wouldn't even know you.

I Am Not Blank

I am not your broken diamond looking glass, I am not your twitter handle, I am not some reflection of yours only female, I am not your access to light or sleep or entertainment. I am not here to enhance your life, I am not your list maker, I am not angry. I am not a means to an end, a comma or a date. I am not a file, a category of nose, a scent in the air. I reject this being pressed into me, onto me, over me. I am not an ink stain to be interpreted. I am not cracked, my voice isn't shrill, I am not joking. I am not a flower, the shape of vase, a pulse, a view. I am not to be ground down and re-used as a form of ink for your pen. I am not a signatory, I never signed in, on or up for this. I am not a looker, I am not asking for it. I am not excited by the brunt of what I am saying, I am fired up, I am not a robot, bitcoin, marsupial, or particularly crepuscular. I am not howling at the moon. I am not flying in the face of that moon. I am not a curl, a raindrop, I do not mew or kitten. I am not scratching your eyes out or trying to make you cry. I am not grieving some long-lost hurt that may have been inflicted on me. I am not a heroine, omnipresent, calculating or final. I am not blank. I am not airbrushed. I am not edited, shortened, silenced or shamed …

Punctuation

Everyone as punctuation: you be an apostrophe signalling
something missing or something owned. I take an umlaut—
mischievous, drawing vowels down unexpected avenues of voice,
a misdirected colon appearing occasionally like a strict but naïve
afterthought; almost impossible to find on the keyboard, but so
easy to add by hand.

I think of my mother as that Spanish question mark, the kind
that precedes the question and appears inverted—¿ a signal before
the rise and rise of the question-song? Looking about the room:
an interrobang; a comma; indices leaning heads together, an
ellipse…

There, another sits, the full stop.

Suspicious Message

A suspicious message came from the deep north with swearing attached: fungal growth, decorations made by disease. Opening it, there was a stink of old rage, worse for ageing; bad cheese grown ancient in its own rancid, caked envelope. I remember *ugly as death's daughter* and *your face a second-hand handkerchief, look hard into the mirror and see how you have degraded* flags waving in a wind of expectation. Although there was a morsel of originality, it still hurt, just as blunt arrows can still burrow under skin. They had lodged there before, scars just pinkly healing, nerves furrowing to grow new sensors for danger. But, these recently defrosted words were rotting under my eyes, breaking and maggoted they crawled away to future places to be digested. I turned to the mirror and saw death's daughter hunted there, her teeth a prickle of white where her smile recognised her. The lichens of her hair, the flags of her lips.

Two Cassandra Poems

1. Cassandra

Consider the prick of tears
in Cassandra's eyes and the fizz
of electricity in the roots of her
hair
when, looking as you would around the corner
or further
down the lane
she would see
inevitable events
chained to time; seconds linking to
seconds like sidle scales
of fish or
ringed armour against
the chests of her Trojan brothers.

Who did she love the most? She had to
catch herself in this thought: because
it wasn't the gold-skinned Apollo
who sought to have her—
to plough her
human flesh
with his own
Godliness until
all the scales would fall from her;
the toughened skin of her feet
the ledges of nail

on her fingers—
until her bones would no longer
be bones but powdered
calcium.

And seeing this
all chains led
to her dusted
from the shoes of armies.
Beauty to desire, desire
to death-fall
no matter how much wisdom was
applied to the wound
insight, even prophecy:
shipwrecked.
Would you choose to be believed if
all you saw was destruction's map?
Athena no solace
the era ending
mythic time askance
the scale of it.

Cassandra needed to
be careful where her thoughts went
or she would know what
was about to happen.
Feeling her virtue and intention grow
cold against the violence
of her heart—
long years plummeting
against that clock in her
body;

she knew before
she uttered a word
that everything she said
was beyond belief.

2. God Kissed

He saw war come in from the ocean but was never accused of listening to snakes in the temple.

His prophecies were cast in limelight.

Cassandra had believed Apollo who washed wrongs clear, dance-flowed through the oracle on Crete. As soon as he gifted her foresight she turned him away—with new laser-truth she saw she could not believe him—shimmering blue hiss—worse would happen from his lust than anything he could install in the mainframe. Apollo—spurned at the entrance of all wonder, which is a woman to a god—kissed into Cassandra new shifting eyes that cried distrust and a forked tongue that curved her words lisp-wards: the more she spoke the more she was defiled. So, tearing her hair from its roots, the new future mapped out below her like the tilled fields of her childhood, she fled.

Helenus, her brother and twin—though he saw truth in a spotlight—would not wash her with his tears.

Kate Bush Quartet

1. Babushka

'Chernobyl was the site of the world's worst nuclear accident and,
for the past 27 years, the area around the plant has been known as
the Exclusion Zone. And yet, a community of about 200 people live
there—almost all of them elderly women. These proud grandmas defied
orders to relocate because their connection to their homeland and to their
community are "forces that rival even radiation."' Holly Morris, Ted
Talk 'Why stay in Chernobyl? Because it's home', October 2013.

One

Blushed as fine as an eyelash
a guarded expression from an era
back in Chernobyl when women were skirted
one after the other, testing the mettle
of men they loved, desired, craved,
skirts hiding so many possibilities
having an underneath where generations of women might crouch
knotted into their very DNA so
any of them could become the other,

and no one could tell.

Two

And how he was before he had met her
how she was before years left tidemarks on her face and hips
how she was before she'd known that he existed
how she was before the tide came in
how she was before she burnt with rage
when she lost her temper, her daily grace, her faith in love

all goodness she'd thought of in the world.
Before her hair fell out
her hips opened up
her lips were a snarl
her eyes were sharp
before he had given the highwayman his diamond betrothal ring
on the road to Chernobyl.

Three

These Soviet dolls have horsehair fine eyes;
lips that knew cherry-glut;
mitochondrial DNA that goes back
to times before 'Made in the USSR'—
and in tightening of their wooden joins
(where they would have kept their knees
if they were not given over to hiding places
for sister/sister/mother/aunt/grandmother…)
they squeak like wingless, featherless birds.

Four

But she had been entrapped so long she didn't see
a jaw on her heel, chain pegged in soil
blue where the teeth took on the skin-bruise
oval bite-mark so familiar she wasn't aware
of it, keeping her down, keeping her there, holding her firm
safely embracing her so she wouldn't get lost or
hurt in the woods of Chernobyl where the trees
knot together like Grandmother's knuckles, and are
as wild as wild as she will not have a chance to be.

2. Running Up That Hill

An Acrostic Poem

Inhale, the air smells like 1981 and here in the binary there is no
    mistaking this offer:
From this moment I'll take your place, you take mine, and then we'll
    see, angel, if it does hurt.

Instantly whatever God heard it, loved this idea—and now, it's you
    here in my costume, performing gender like a songstress.

On your lips, a painted smile
Narrowed into concentration
Like a surprise that runs from your toes right up the hill—
You didn't know about the deal I was making?

Can you inhale a view from the top of that hill?
Out over the horizon unmistakable signs of certainty
Uttering a coded cry, the experience
Like nothing ever before or after
Dimming down any promise to behave like you...

My Face is as fresh as 1981, like icecaps
And the snow on the mountains that has not melted
Knifing its way down the slope,
Erosion defaces the whole panorama.

A deal is a deal is a deal, sweetheart.

Don't you see, we are programmed, messages that mistake
Each to each? Singing like a girl caged in the body of a girl
Arrow knocked in her string.
Let me steal this moment from you. Now.

Will we change to our original selves?
In the deal, was there a clause, an option, a way to default?
This is no joke, but it does seem to be hurting you,
Helpings of experience at full tilt.

Gods must listen to the radio, you see,
Only they took me seriously this time
Down to the very way we both matter.

3. Hounds of Love

I recognised myself just through there:
in the forest's heartbeat the branch-angle
deep-lake refraction dark water.

If I know I am a coward then I have seen
something that means that I am not afraid.
I recognise myself just through there in

the wolf-call distance, urgent to finish this singing
stalked in shadow-beams, in tree fork
while I recognise part of me just over there—

spangled all over with fears I have pulled through
childhood; all the way from the safety
of knowing that I was a coward and seeing

that it was me, all along in risks between
the fury of the pack and my own cracking jaw
biting down on myself, afraid of being this coward

I saw who loved me better that way.
Reflected in the forest, the yawn of dark.
Refracted and shattered into song.

4. Voice

Up high there is an ice cold tinge
take it up to ghost, take it up beyond pan's pipes
take it to a plateau where mist falls off sound,
curls into broken-open, melts.

Then, down she comes, swooping and birdlike.
We fall in love with the warm richness of red-tones
where she is older; where she lands to explain her earlier flutes
were all about recent past, were all morning time greeting

and now she can reveal the whole of herself
lowering the tone, taking it down to vibrato,
bass in the wood, breaks open in a new solo
where high notes tremble in memory and haunt
down here on the earth she is as possible.

Ophiuchus

Three hundred and ninety million light years away Ophiuchus'
curved edge revealed a cavity so large it drew in matter and then,
material, energy, things yet unnamed and unswallowed erupted
in unprecedented explosive force taking over space enough for
fifteen of our Milky Ways to spread their arms and spirals against
the black.

Notes

'Haven in Lost: A Song' was witten as part of community lockdown project 'Write to Me': an initiative of the YouAreHere festival and Ainslie+Gorman Arts Centre where a set of multidisciplinary artists responded to postcards sent in with stories of lost objects.

'Nadya Ngambri—Also Known as Mount Ainslie': *Nadya* translates to *Mother* in the Nyamudy language of the Canberra region.

Some of the poems in this collection have been previously published as follows:

'Corpus Callosum as Erosion' and an earlier version of 'Will It Snow Tonight' and 'All My Troubles'—*Axon Journal,* On the Mend: Care, repair & breakage, Dec 2021

'Currency'—*Arc Magazine*, 2022

'Babushka'—*Meniscus* 2023

'Haiku/ How the Plastic Bag Was Not A Crow'—*Authoria Magazine* 2023

'Haven For the Lost: A song—Commissioned for Post Art lockdown initiative', You Are Here Festival, 2020

'Amongst the Messy Scrub'—Commissioned for 'Myicelium Sky' Paul Summerfield's 2023 solo exhibition, Belconnen Arts centre, Feb 2023.

'Kate Bush Quartet'—Written and Performed for *Wuthering Nights*, a multidisciplinary show, March 2023.

Acknowledgements

This book owes thanks to many facets of my life. Thanks are due to Felicity Plunkett and the team at Varuna as well as the Poetry Master Class participants who workshopped early drafts of many of these poems. Thanks to the team at Ainslie+Gorman who make my writing studio into a home, and the other residents whose dedication to your craft and manifold arts communities inspire my own. Thanks to the Prose Poetry Collective who generously share their work into my inbox and who have seen many of the poems in early stages. Thanks to Cathy Tippet and the team at Dementia Australia who supported me and facilitated my learning at the difficult period of time this book was born and for running the course on frontal lobe dementia that really aided my insight and understanding of the patterns that were occurring in my life. The beautiful and diverse Blue Gum Community School family have been a resource of glimmering joy and inspiration. Also, my own real life family Winston, Toby, Aoife, Lockie and Maya as well as the pets are my deep true life that I love without reserve or measure. Thanks to my parents, Wendy and Mark, who put the arts at the forefront of my early life. Special thanks to the friends who listened to the woes. To Virginia Cook for her patronage of the CAPO Cook Creative Writing Award, which I received in 2022. To Penelope Layland for her keen and kind editorial work on this manuscript. To beautiful Kirsten Biven, who provided 'Katie's Chair' as exquisite cover art. Thanks to my poet friends and friends who are artists, those who were able to get involved in my Insta experiments. Special thanks to Shane Strange for his work on this and all the variously delicious Recent Work poetry books.

About the Author

Lucy Alexander is a poet and writer working on Ngunnawal/Ngambri land, where she's a resident at the vibrant Ainslie and Gorman Arts Centre. At the beginning of lockdown in 2020 *Strokes of Light* was released by Recent Work Press. *Equations of Breath* is her fourth collection of poems. Lucy's poetry is published in journals, recently appearing in *Meniscus* and *Authoria*, as well as being anthologised and also read on radio at ArtsSoundFM. She was the recipient of the CAPO Cook Creative Writing Award in 2022, as well as a participant in Varuna's masterclasses with Felicity Plunkett. She teaches and builds word constructions as well as juggling delightful and challenging family life.

Cover image: 'Katie's Chair' © Kirsten Biven, 2024,
Instagram: kirstenbachbiven

www.ingramcontent.com/pod-product-compliance
Ingram Content Group Australia Pty Ltd
76 Discovery Rd, Dandenong South VIC 3175, AU
AUHW020639050325
407891AU00002B/10

9 780645 973259